The Care

Of Guinea Pigs
Handbook

Alkeith O Jackson

The Care Of Guinea Pigs Handbook

Housing, Feeding, Breeding And Diseases

Alkeith O Jackson

3

Copyright Notice

Disclaimer and Terms of Use

This book is a general educational health-related information product. As an express condition to reading this book, you understand and agree to the following terms. The books content is not a substitute for direct, personal, professional medical care and diagnosis.

The Author and/ or Publisher of this book is not responsible in any manner whatsoever for any consequential damages that result from the use of, or the inability to use this book.

First Printing, 2014

ISBN-13: 978-1500659349

Contents

Preface: How to Care For Your Guinea Pig

Whether you are new to guinea pig care or are an experienced owner, there is always something new for you to learn about these cute and delicate pets. Guinea pigs -- also known as the cavy make great pets because they can live in just about any homes, whether it's a suburban home or city apartments.

No matter who you are or where you live, guinea pigs are a fun and rewarding pet to have around. Don't be scared: although guinea pigs need continual care and attention, they are not as demanding as some other popular pets, making them perfect for older children or people with busy lives.

On average, they live up to about eight years, so they will be a long-term commitment and not just short-term. But if proper care is given; your New Guinea Pig, will be around for a very long time. Well-known for their cute sounds, guinea pigs are very intelligent and are capable of communicating their needs to their owners. And of course, guinea pigs, like any other pet, have needs. At this point you may be wondering what those needs are and how much they cost, right?

One of the most amazing things about these delicate creatures is that they don't require much investment at all. Many countries around the world, including the US, have severe animal overpopulation problems.

These shelters also carry cavy (guinea pigs,) as they may have been rescued or dropped off for care. Since guinea pigs are more difficult for shelters to unload, they often offer the animals for completely free. So not only could you save an animal's life, but you could also get it for free!

Like anyone else, guinea pigs love eating. You may discover that your new guinea pig eats (or grazes) all the time. What do they eat? Most guinea pigs are good with hay, fresh water, and guinea pig pellets.

It is very important that your pet have these items at all times. However, they are not expensive. You will also want to give them some vegetables and the occasional fruit snack. Like us, guinea pigs can't provide their own vitamin C, so it's up to their owners to give it to them to eat. Yes, guinea pigs are strict herbivores - never try to give them meat.

Another important thing that you need to know about guinea pigs is that they are social creatures who want to live in herds. This means, you will need to get at least two guinea pigs living together and not just one.

Even if you give them a companion, you'll need to spend some time with them every day. However, their lives are more fulfilling if they can spend most of their day with their own kind. Since they are delicate animals, you will also want to watch their health closely. Guinea pigs are prey animals. This means they are programmed to hide their illnesses and pain from you as they would in the wild.

As you can imagine, a sick guinea pig can deteriorates very fast. That's why it's important to watch out for signs of a sick cavy. You can regularly weigh them and take them to the vet.

Another thing to keep in mind is that guinea pigs need a large cage to run, jump, sleep, play, and leave their waste in. As we mentioned before, they are prey animals, and thus feel most content being able to hide somewhere either from their own kind or humans. Small houses are popular in pet stores and can be purchase for a reasonable price.

After you purchase a suitable house for your guinea pig, you only need to provide some chicken coop flooring, their water bottle, and some feeding materials to get your guinea pig ready to move in.

Introduction

Guinea Pigs And Their Relatives

The name of guinea-pigs which is given to these little creatures is really misleading, for they are not related to pigs and did not originate in either Guinea or New Guinea. They are properly cavies, and though no naturalist can state definitely from what particular species they are descended, there is

11

no doubt that they originated in Central or South America, where numerous wild varieties of their family still exist.

Cavies are very easily reared and are so docile, quiet, good-natured, and neat that they are universal favorites with kids and fanciers. Although mainly used as pets, or for exhibition purposes, many people keep them to drive away rats and mice; for it is a common belief—apparently founded on fact— that rats and mice will not infest buildings or houses where cavies are confined.

The commonest type, or breed, of cavy is a smooth haired variety known as the English or Bolivian Cavy. These are found in a great variety of colors and are divided by fanciers into several distinct classes for exhibition purposes. The most important are Bolivian Solt-Colored Cavies.

The main points in this variety are the large head with an outward curve to the face, or "Roman nose"; fairly large ears turned over at the upper edge and nearly bare of hair; short neck; deep, wide shoulders; broad back; and a plentiful, short, soft, glossy coat.

The main point to be obtained is an even coloring of a single shade of red, cream, brown, black, or white. A single hair of any other color will disqualify this breed for prize contests, and only by constant care in breeding and the elimination of all parti-colored stock can good results be obtained.

Chapter 1

Handling Your Guinea Pig

You should make sure your guinea pig can see you when you approach it.

- Talk to it in a soft voice and stroke it gently.

- Put one hand on its front chest, and use the other hand to support it from the back.

- Hold the cavy close to your chest while supporting it with both of your hands.

- Hold onto it firmly, but never squeeze it. Guinea pigs have fragile internal organs.

15

- If it starts to struggle, move down to the floor to prevent your guinea pig from falling.

Owners should handle their guinea pig as much as they can so that they can bond with each other. It's equally important to spend time talking to their guinea pig and giving it treats in order to build up trust.

How Much Time Should You Spend Handling Your Guinea Pig?

- It's best not to hold your guinea pig for more than 15 minutes. Otherwise, you may keep it from using the bathroom.

- If your pet wants to be put down sooner, it will communicate with you by whining or biting at your clothes.

- It's not uncommon for a guinea pig to defecate on its owner. If held too long, guinea pigs may also urinate on their owners.

What Not to Do When Touching Your Guinea Pig

Like people, every guinea pig has spots it likes to be touched and spots where it doesn't want to be touched. It's important to pay attention to your guinea pig and learn their preferred spots.

Most guinea pigs do not want to be touched on their stomach or their rear. However, nearly all cavies enjoy being stroked on the head, right between the ears. Many pets also enjoy being rubbed on their neck beneath the chin.

Returning Your Guinea Pig to Its Cage

It's important to make sure you have a solid hold on your cavy before you put it back in its cage. Sometimes guinea pigs struggle when you hold them, but if you use the technique outlined above, they'll adjust.

After a few weeks, you should see real progress. Even when they're being cooperative, pets often begin to squirm when they get close to the cage floor. If your pet

17

does this, hold it firmly just above the floor until it calms down. Allow it to touch the cage floor, but don't let it go until it stops struggling completely. This is a good way to ensure a cavy isn't injured when being returned to its cage. It's effective even when done by smaller children.

Chapter 2

What to Do If Your Cavy Escapes

Every now and then, a cavy gets out of its cage. If this happens, there are several things you can do. Before you begin your search, make sure it isn't just hiding in the cage.

- Start by blocking of all escape exits.

- Next, look in its usual hiding places.

- If you haven't seen it, try luring it out of hiding with food.

- Be patient with your cavy.

- It may bite when you try to pick it up after hiding, but it will get used to being held in time.

What to Do If Your Cavy Gets Pregnant

- If a guinea pig becomes pregnant, it will require additional levels of care.

- It's important to take her to see the veterinarian right away.

- It's best not to handle the guinea pig much late in the pregnancy. It's especially important not to hold your pet near the neck, as this can cause her to miscarry her babies.

- If your guinea pig does need to be transported, do it in a box that has openings that let in light and air.

- Be patient, and take extra precautions whenever possible.

Once your guinea pig is 3 to 4 weeks into her pregnancy, she'll need to be placed in an area separate from male guinea pigs.

Otherwise, the male cavy may try to mount the female, which could hurt both her and her babies. It's also possible that she could become impregnated right after giving birth, which could be quite harmful.

After to 4 to 5 weeks, your guinea pig should be place in a nursery alone. This nursery should be at least 8 square feet, and should be both warm and quiet. It should contain all the toys and food your cavy will need.

You'll also want to give your guinea pig more vegetables to eat, especially foods that are rich in vitamin C. Alfalfa pellets and alfalfa hay are also excellent choices. This contains extra protein, calcium, and carbohydrates, and is designed specifically for pregnant guinea pigs and their pups. It shouldn't be given to other guinea pigs.

Handling Babies

When cavies are first born, they'll need time to adjust to the world. In order to avoid trauma, owners should not do the following things:

- Cuddle them
- Make loud noises

Lurk or loom over them. The babies may see the owner as a predator, which will trigger their instinct to run and hide. Instead, when you observe the babies, you should put yourself at their eye level.

In regards to other pets, it's best to keep them away from the babies for a few days. After that, you can introduce them individually.

Chapter 3

Guinea Pig Care and Housing

Cavies require comparatively little space, for they are not particularly active creatures, but their hutches should be large enough to afford plenty of space for moving freely about, and in good weather they should be placed in pens or boxes, with a wire-netting top and no bottom, which may stand on a plot of grass. Regular feeding, cleanliness, and proper food and bedding are the most important points.

While quite hardy, cavies should not be kept out-of-doors in cold weather but should be housed in a fairly warm building and given plenty of clean straw, although with the shorthaired varieties, sawdust, peat, or dry sand will keep the hutches free from moisture and is easily replaced when dirty. Long-haired cavies frequently nibble each other's hair, and for this reason the Peruvians should be kept in separate hutches. The other varieties may be kept in hutches holding several individuals, but the does and bucks, over five or six weeks old, should be separated.

Chapter 4

Guinea Pig Feeding

Cavies will eat almost anything of a vegetable nature; but they are often overfed or improperly fed, and it is a good rule to feed only the best and just enough. Sweet hay should be given morning and evening, and if a little hay is always in the hutch it will do no harm and will give the creatures something to nibble at.

Hay should be placed in a rack within easy reach, for if scattered loose in the cage or hutch it will be trodden and soiled and of no use as food. Bread and milk, squeezed almost dry, is good with the morning meal, as are also a few large oats. For the midday feed green food is advisable, such as plantains, watercress, carrot tops, parsley, dandelions, chicory, and clover.

Every few days a slight change in diet should be made, and the evening meal should regularly include a mixture of bran, meal, oats, barley, or rice made just moist enough to stick together. By a little experimenting you can soon determine just how much food should be given at each meal, and you should try to give just enough to satisfy the animals without leaving any appreciable waste.

Never place the food loose in the hutch, but set it in little dishes or pans with a broad bottom which cannot be readily upset. Cavies as a rule do not drink much but depend upon the natural moisture in green food; but a little clean water should always be provided.

Chapter 5

Proteins, Carbs, Vitamins and Minerals

Proteins, carbs, vitamins, minerals, (especially water) are the most necessary nutrients for your cavy. Mix them carefully so your pet can have a well-balanced diet.

- Water
- Grass Hay
- Pellets (the two above items are more important.)
- Occasional fruits
- Daily vegetables full of vitamins
- Vitamin C supplements should be given to your guinea pig, (if it is not getting sufficient amount through their daily diets.)

Guinea pigs are delicate eaters with an even more delicate digestive system. When introducing new food, try to do it slowly until they have built up a tolerance. If they like a small piece, gradually increase the serving size every day.

It is also recommended that you provide your pets with the following healthy nutrients and organic foods:

Water

Some people can use untreated tap water, but you should have it tested to make sure there is no chlorine or other additives that can harm your pet.

Distilled water does not offer the necessary nutrients needed, so avoid it. As bacteria can form easily from what's in your guinea pig's mouth, always keep the nozzle on your drip bottle clean. Avoid water high in certain minerals, such as calcium.

Get unflavored drinking water or water fresh from a spring. Provide the water in a cage-mounted drip bottle, not a standing dish. This way you avoid spills and any contamination. Guinea pigs need to have regular access to clean; fresh water with no frills added and that is replenished daily.

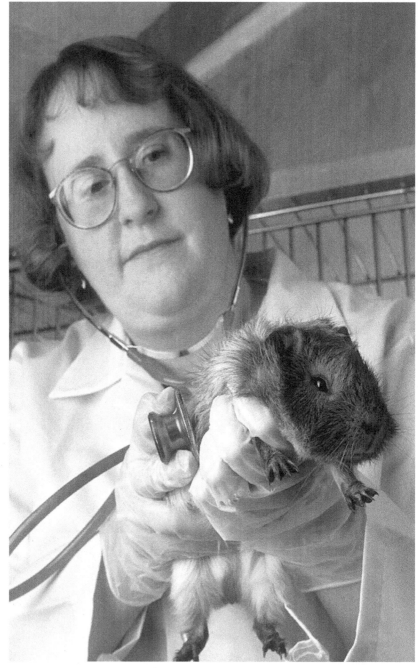

Chapter 6

Taking Proper Care of Your Guinea Pig

Taking proper care of your guinea pig is important. Follow the instructions below to ensure your pet has all of the care it needs. Hay does not cause any concerning increase in guinea pig weight. This food source does provide some nutrients for them, including protein.

Hay

As grazing animals, your guinea pig will want an unlimited supply of grass hay for two reasons.

33

The long hay strands keeps the guinea pig gastrointestinal system moving, which is good health for them. The teeth of a cavy are constantly growing, and chewing hay helps grind them down.

Shopping for hay is best done locally. A nearby farm that sells that from fresh grass is preferable. You should smell it first. Good hay will have a pleasant odor and a green tint. Many animals will not eat hay that has not been handled properly. If it has no smell or an off-putting odor, do not buy it. You should also avoid hay that is brown or has dust on it.

One mistake some people make is purchasing straw when they intend to get hay. Straw provides almost no nutrients. It is brown and much firmer than the preferred hay. Hay is generally classified into two classes. It is necessary to understand each and the differences prior to purchase.

The first is grass hay. This should be available to your pet at all times. The most common choice of grass hay sold in stores is Timothy hay.

The other type of hay that is commonly fed to guinea pigs is legume hay. This is a dietary supplement that should only be used under certain conditions. Otherwise, the high amounts of calcium in it may cause bladder stones in your pet.

However, guinea pigs that are pregnant or ill can benefit from the additional calcium. The high levels of carbs and proteins are also ideal for young guinea pigs. The most common type is alfalfa.

Pellets

This is a great way to supplement hay when feeding your guinea pigs. Each of your pets should have between one-eighth and one-quarter of a cup pellets per serving. Make certain they are specifically for guinea pigs and are free from dyes.

To keep the food from being tipped over, the pellets should be placed in a bottom heavy rodent serving dish. To maximize the health of your pet, look for a pellet product that has been fortified with vitamin C.

In order to maintain the vitamin content of the pellets, they should be stored in an airtight container. Place it in a dark location that is cool and free from moisture. As with human foodstuffs, check for the expiration date prior to purchase.

While it may be tempting to feed your pet any pellet food on the market that is appropriately sized, this is unwise. The nutritional values are not the same and may harm your pet. The whimsically colored pellets are often attractive to pet owners but, should be avoided due to all of the chemicals.

It is best to stick with the monotone ones instead.

Chapter 7

Vegetable Selection

When it comes to veggies, green leafy vegetables are a must. Certain items should only be given every few days and, others are ideal for feedings throughout the day. Any uneaten food should be removed from the cage. If produce is on the verge of spoiling, it should never be fed to your pet.

Vary the selection of vegetables you feed your guinea pig for maximum nutritional value. Make certain the foods are not frozen or very cold when presented to your pet or it may cause diarrhea.

You should never give your pet iceberg lettuce. It has little nutritional value and the nitrates are not good for the animal. Avoid anything from the cabbage family to avoid bloating. Also, beet greens should not be fed to your guinea pig.

Ideal vegetables to feed your guinea pig include carrots and deseeded bell peppers. Green and yellow peppers are recommended. All parts of the carrot can be fed to your pet, be careful not to overfeed the root portion. Cucumbers are low in nutrition but, the high water levels make them beneficial, especially during warm months.

Lettuces that can be fed daily to guinea pigs include green and red leaf, butter-head, and romaine. Curly and Belgian endive are flavorful treats for your pet, as are Swiss chard and chicory greens.

Artichokes, arugula, and dill can be consumed regularly. Zucchini is a nice change of pace for your pet as well.

A couple of times a week, you can give your pet red or orange bell peppers that have had the seeds removed. Asparagus is a delicious treat they are certain to appreciate, as are basil and green leek tops. Pumpkin can be fed to your pet but, care must be taken to remove all of the seeds first.

Small portions of spinach can be served to your pet, as can thyme and watercress. Because they are part of the cabbage family, broccoli and cauliflower should be given in tiny doses as well. The same goes for kale and Chinese cabbage.

Celery leaves can be fed to your pet, as can the stalks. However, the stalks need to be cut up to minimize the choking hazard of the stringy portions.

Grass that is free from chemicals and has not been defecated on by other animals is a flavorful and natural treat. Tomatoes can be served, providing that the green top and seeds have been carefully removed first.

Fruits are a great supplement to the diet of your pet. Care should be taken in the selection and preparation of these treats to keep sugar and acidity levels in check. One-eighth of a regular size piece of fruit, supplied every three to four days is sufficient to meet the requirements of your guinea pig.

Dried fruits can be fed to them. However, due to the concentration of sugars, the dosage should be even smaller than for fresh fruits and only provided once or twice each month.

Moderate amounts of bananas are beneficial, as are thin slices of peel containing apples. The seeds must be removed from apples prior to serving.

Grapefruit and cranberries are excellent sources of vitamin C. Strawberries and oranges are delicious options, as are strawberries and seedless grapes. You may also want to consider a few blueberries or blackberries to vary the nutritional content of your pet diet.

Chapter 8

Breeding

Although cavies will breed at a very early age, the young will be stronger and better if the old ones are kept separated until eight or nine months old. Peruvians used for breeding purposes should have the hair clipped quite short, as it is likely to become matted and dirty if not combed, and to do this when the doe has young is not advisable.

Moreover, the long hair is a great impediment to the mother when nursing her young, and as breeding animals are not shown in exhibitions, the loss of hair is immaterial.

The young cavies should be left with the mother for four or five weeks. Then they will begin to eat solid food, and during this time plenty of warm mash, bread and milk, and crushed oats should be fed. If you are raising stock for exhibition, the young that do not approach a standard should be disposed of for pets or to other breeders, and only the really good ones retained.

Cavies are very prolific, and a great difficulty is in keeping down the stock and maintaining perfectly marked or standard individuals. In selecting does and bucks, or, as sometimes called, "sows and boars" for breeding, you should choose does having good size and coats and select the bucks which possess the best characters lacking in the does, such as color, form, eyes, etc.

Chapter 9

Diseases

Cavies are free from all vermin and are not at all subject to disease or parasites of any kind. Snuffles, pot-bellies, loose bowels, and epileptic fits are sometimes met with, however. These troubles are caused mainly by lack of cleanliness, improper food, or sudden changes in temperature and should be cured as far as possible by natural means.

Less food, especially green food, and more exercise will usually remedy a "pot-belly," while even temperature and plenty of warm bedding will cure colds or "snuffles." Fits usually result in death but can be avoided by not overfeeding with rich food.

Chapter 10

Different Types Of Cavies

Bolivian Agouti Cavies

This is a well-marked variety of the common cavy in which the short, glossy hair is a beautiful silver-gray, with black "tickings" through the hair and known as "Silver-Grays," or else the color is rich golden-yellow beneath, with black "tickings" over the head, legs, and feet. This form is known as the "Golden Agouti" and is a very handsome and attractive variety.

Bolivian Tortoise-Shell Cavies

To stand a chance of prize winning this type should have but three colors—red, black, and yellow—and while the colors may be arranged in any pattern or proportion, they should be sharply defined and should never blend or mix.

White spots or patches should not be permitted, for the animals thus marked belong in another class, known as "Tortoise-Shells and Whites." These should, as a rule, have less white than tortoise-shell colors, and the white markings should be as regular and evenly distributed as possible.

Bolivian Dutch-Marked Cavies

These are cavies in which white with red, black with white, yellow with white, or similar colors are distributed much in the same manner as a Dutch-marked rabbit, or, in other words, in heavy, regular blotches, with distinct, sharp edges. Specimens marked unequally on both sides will not prove prize winners but may be excellent to breed from.

Interesting and lovable as are the common Bolivian Cavies, other more fancy varieties are even more attractive. Prominent among these are the Peruvians and Abyssinians, neither of which names have anything to do with the native country of these little creatures, which are merely varieties or breeds of the commonplace guinea-pig.

Peruvian Cavies

These are very striking-looking creatures when well bred, and the greatest difficulty is often found in distinguishing head from tail, so heavily covered and completely concealed are the little fellows by the enormously long, silky hair.

Peruvians are not as hardy as the Bolivians and require daily brushing to keep their coats in good condition. The best way to accomplish this is to hold the cavy on the palm of the left hand and brush the hair with a common hair-brush. A wire brush or comb should never be used for this purpose.

This is a breed particularly well adapted for rearing by girls, and many of the best prize winners in this class have been exhibited by girls. The main point to be gained in the Peruvian Cavy is a broad, flattish body and very long, silky, abundant hair, which should touch the ground on the sides and trail behind and should completely cover the face, much as in the Yorkshire terrier. Color is of little importance, for they are shown in blacks, blues, grays, white, yellows, browns, and in various combinations of these colors.

Abyssinian Cavies

This is considered the hardiest variety of all cavies, and they are so odd and peculiar in appearance that every cavy fancier should raise them. While the coat of a Peruvian should be as silky as possible, the hair of an Abyssinian should be as harsh or rough as possible.

Secondary to the harshness of the fur is the matter of "rosettes." These are little circular, star-like growths of hair dotted all over the head and body, which give the rumpled and brushed-the-wrong-way effect. The short, bristly hair on the face and lips gives this breed the appearance of being quite ferocious, but in reality they are as gentle and quiet as any other variety. Color in this breed is not important, although the solid or "self" colors and tortoiseshells are very attractive.

Animals Related to the Guinea-Pig

Although the original ancestor of the domestic guinea-pig is not known with certainty, yet there are many species of cavy-like creatures found wild in tropical America, and nearly all of these are easily tamed and become as gentle and affectionate as the true guinea-pig.

There are also quite a number of animals closely related to guinea-pigs, yet very different in appearance and in their habits, which are, nevertheless, subject to practically the same treatment, feeding, and housing.

While these various unusual animals are not always to be found in the stores of animal dealers or fanciers, yet now and then you may come across one of them, and sailors returning from trips often bring them home.

As out-of-the-way pets always attract attention and are interesting, it is advisable to secure such specimens when you can, especially if you raise other animals such as guinea-pigs, rabbits, squirrels, etc. As a rule, all these creatures are low in price, for comparatively few dealers know anything of their habits or needs and are glad to get rid of them.

There is no trouble in disposing of them to zoological gardens or menageries if in good condition, should you wish to do so, and in the meantime you can learn a lot about their habits and peculiarities; while if they breed in captivity you may often make a good profit from the original outlay.

Agoutis

These animals are natives of South and Central America and the West Indies and, while seldom seen in captivity in this country, yet in their native lands they are often seen in confinement and make very attractive, interesting, and intelligent pets, and are great favorites with the natives.

They are closely related to the guinea-pigs, being a species of wild cavy, and in general form they resemble these well-known animals. They are a lot larger, however, often measuring 2 feet in length, and have longer legs, a heavier head, and hoof-like claws.

There are several species but, while differing slightly in the length of the tiny tail and in color, all are very much alike. In color they are brownish, more or less "ticked" or dotted with various shades of yellow, reddish, or gray, and with reddish or rich golden-yellow on the rump and legs.

The hair is rather coarse but thick, and is very long on the rump, which gives the agouti a queer, "tucked-in-behind" appearance. Agoutis live naturally in deep woods and feed mainly at night, but in captivity they behave very much like guinea-pigs.

They have strong, chisel-like teeth, and are constantly gnawing at something and, unless provided with bits of sticks or roots, will gnaw their houses or cages to pieces. Agoutis eat almost anything in the way of vegetable food, but they are particularly fond of roots, bark, and corn-stalks, and do not care so much for cabbage, lettuce, or grass as do other members of the family.

Their general care is much like that described for guinea-pigs, but their hutches should be very much larger, and, if allowed to run in an enclosure, care should be taken to have the surrounding fence extend at least 2 feet beneath the surface, as these animals burrow deeply.

Agoutis breed readily in captivity and usually have two young to a litter. Those born in captivity are usually very tame, and if given perfect freedom will remain close to home and soon learn to come to a call or whistle. They are much more intelligent than domestic cavies and may be taught a number of tricks.

The Pampas Cavy

This is a remarkable species of wild cavy, found in Argentina and Patagonia, and properly known as the Patagonian Cavy, but, owing to this name being more commonly applied to one of the fancy breeds of guinea-pigs, it is confusing.

55

This animal has very long, slender legs and a short tail, and with its prominent ears it looks at first sight like some sort of a rabbit. It is of good size, 2 to 3 feet in length, and weighs as much as twenty-five to thirty pounds. The fur is crisp, short, thick, and rusty yellow in color on the sides and legs, becoming gray on the back, and blackish on the rump, which is also decorated by a broad white band.

The belly is white. These cavies are shy, watchful, restless creatures when wild, but when raised from the young in captivity they become very tame and interesting.

They are seldom seen in the North, even in menageries or zoological gardens, but on the large estancias or ranches of the pampas, one or two are frequently seen about the house or grounds, where they are perfectly at home and are favorite pets with the native children.

The Paca

This is another odd animal related to the cavies and found throughout Central and South America. It is a very handsome little animal about 2 feet long, but stouter and shorter-legged than the agoutis, and with close, short hair.

The color is brownish above and white below, with seven longitudinal bands, or rows, of white spots. It is a retiring animal and naturally nocturnal in its habits. It is very fond of water and swims and dives readily. It is as easy to raise in confinement as the common cavies but should always be given a large pan or tub of water in which to swim in warm weather. The paca eats any sort of vegetable food, but should be provided with more roots and sticks than ordinary cavies.

Capybaras

These are the largest of all the cavy family, and are often 4 feet in length and weigh as much as one hundred pounds. Their heads are so large, heavy, and blunt, their bodies so massive, and their claws so hoof-like that at first sight they appear more like pigs than cavies.

They are exceedingly fond of water, and in their native land—South America—they always take to the water when frightened or attacked. For this reason, they are often known as Water Cavies.

They are quite intelligent and are easily domesticated, but their great size and thin, coarse hair make them unattractive for pets, and they are far better suited for menageries or for collections of foreign animals. Their food and general habits are much like those of their tiny cousins, the guinea-pigs.

Chinchillas

These dainty, soft-furred creatures are closely related to the cavies and guinea-pigs and are easy to keep as pets but seldom breed in confinement. They are natives of Peru and are mountain animals and quite hardy, and will stand our northern climate if housed during the coldest weather. Their food is similar to that of rabbits, cavies, and other rodents.

VISCACHAS

These are animals forming a sort of connecting-link between the bushy-tailed chinchillas and the cavies, and in South America they occupy much the same position as do our western gophers, or ground-squirrels in this country.

Like these, they prove very troublesome at times where abundant and, as they are about feet long, they can do a correspondingly greater amount of damage. In color the Viscachas are gray, mottled with darker gray, white, and yellow, with black bands on the head. They are very easily tamed and become very affectionate. Their food is much like that of cavies, but they are also very fond of roots and of thistles.

Porcupines

These odd, spiny, sluggish creatures are often kept as curiosities, for their prickly nature hardly permits them to be used as pets, although they become fairly tame and are quite easily domesticated. The common American Porcupine lives in all our Northern States and Canada, and is so well able to protect itself that it is seldom molested and becomes quite tame about camps and houses.

The American species is provided with numerous short, slender quills, or spines, which are mostly concealed in the long, thick fur, but the tail, which is short, broad, and blunt, is well covered with spines. The claws are hooked, and the creature climbs large trees readily and frequently entirely strips them of bark.

These creatures are very slow in motion, sluggish, and uninteresting, and should be handled and approached with caution, for the old idea that the porcupine could "shoot" its quills has considerable truth. The animal cannot really "shoot" the quills, but when disturbed the tail is jerked suddenly from side to side and the loosely fastened quills are thus thrown for some distance.

The European Porcupine is a very different-looking creature, with long quills projecting far beyond the hair, and, unlike its American relative, it lives entirely on the ground.

Porcupines eat all sorts of vegetable food, especially roots and bark, and may be kept out-of-doors in runs or enclosures, but the native species will readily climb over netting fences, and for this reason boards leaning inward should extend up for 3 or 4 feet from the ground inside the netting.

1/15-N

CPSIA information can be obtained at www.ICGtesting.com
Printed in the USA
LVOW01s0855171214

419132LV00015BB/341/P